W9-ARX-115

Unsolved Mysteries

Millennium Prophecies

Brian Innes

RSVP
RAINTREE
STECK-VAUGHN
PUBLISHERS
A Steck-Vaughn Company

Austin, Texas

Developed by Brown Partworks
Editor: Lindsey Lowe
Designer: Joan Curtis
Picture Researcher: Brigitte Arora

Raintree Steck-Vaughn Publishers Staff
Project Manager: Joyce Spicer
Editor: Pam Wells

Library of Congress Cataloging-in-Publication Data
Innes, Brian.
 Millennium prophecies/by Brian Innes.
  p. cm.—(Unsolved mysteries)
 Includes bibliographical references and index.
 Summary: Discusses the Western millennium and some of the
prophecies associated with its arrival, from Nostradamus to the Bible code
and Edgar Cayce.
 ISBN 0-8172-5486-2 (Hardcover)
 ISBN 0-8172-5848-5 (Softcover)
 1. Prophecies (Occultism)—Juvenile literature. 2. Millennium—
Miscellanea—Juvenile literature.
 [1. Millennium. 2. Prophecies (Occultism)]
 I. Title. II. Series: Innes, Brian. Unsolved mysteries.
 BF1791.I58 1999
 133.3—dc21   98-27576
             CIP
             AC

Printed and bound in the United States
1 2 3 4 5 6 7 8 9 0 WZ 02 01 00 99 98

Acknowledgments

Cover: John Warden/Tony Stone Images; **Page 5:**
Erich Lessing/AKG London; **Page 6:** Gianni Dagli
Orti/Corbis; **Page 7:** Kevin Morris/Corbis; **Page 9:**
E.T. Archive; **Page 10:** Mary Evans Picture Library;
Page 11: Erich Lessing/AKG London; **Page 13:** Peter
Turnley/Corbis; **Page 15:** Scheufler Collection/
Corbis; **Page 17:** Historical Picture Archive/Corbis;
Page 19: UPI/Corbis-Bettmann; **Page 21:** USGS-
Hawaii Volcano Observatory/Corbis; **Page 23:** Dave
Bartruff/Corbis; **Page 25:** Francoise de Mulder/
Corbis; **Page 26:** David H. Wells/Corbis;

Page 27: Richard T. Nowitz/Corbis; **Page 29:**
Corbis-Bettmann; **Page 30:** Paolo Ragazzini/Corbis;
Page 32: (left) Michael St. Maur Sheil/Corbis,
(right) Carol Havens/Corbis; **Page 33:** Dennis di
Cicco/Corbis; **Page 35:** Richard T. Nowitz/
Corbis; **Page 36:** Yann Arthus-Bertrand/Corbis;
Page 37: Hulton-Deutsch Collection/Corbis;
Page 39: Fortean Picture Library; **Page 40:** Francoise
de Mulder/ Corbis; **Page 41:** Chuck Kuhn/Image
Bank; **Page 43:** AKG London; **Page 45:** Richard
T. Nowitz/Corbis.

Contents

What Is the Millennium?

With the turn of the century on January 1, 2000, we will enter a new millennium. But what does this mean?

This is a page from a 9th-century book (opposite). It is an early type of farming calendar. Each picture shows the work that needs to be done in that month.

The word *millennium* comes from Latin and means "1,000 years." Most people are interested in numbers, and everybody feels that 1,000 is a particularly important number.

The idea of the almost mysterious importance of numbers goes back to at least the 6th century B.C. This was during the time of the great Greek thinker and mathematician named Pythagoras. Pythagoras used numbers to come up with the basis of geometry. This is the branch of math that deals with lines, angles, and shapes, such as squares and circles. However, as well as solving math problems, numbers seem to be particularly important when they mark the passing of time.

THE PASSING OF TIME

In order to make sense of time, years are divided into 12 months, and months into 7-day weeks. One hundred years make a century. Somehow each century seems to have its own character. People talk about "19th-century architecture," or "20th-century progress."

The passing of 1,000 years—ten centuries—has a particular meaning to it. To many people the year 2000 represents a very important milestone.

In order to make sense of time, years are divided into 12 months, and months into . . . weeks.

This is an Aztec calendar. The Aztecs were an ancient civilization in Mexico. They were defeated by the Spanish in the 1500s.

In the new century, people hope to leave behind all the troubles and mistakes of the 20th century. They hope for a better future in the 21st century.

In past centuries some people believed that the year 2000 would mark the beginning of a "golden age" of peace and worldwide prosperity. On the other hand, many more believed that the year 2000 would see the end of the world. There are those who still believe this. However, it is only in the Christian calendar that the year is numbered 2000. Other faiths, or people with different religious beliefs, number their years differently. Even the lengths of their years are measured in different ways. This millennium—the year 2000—does not have the same importance for them.

OTHER CALENDARS

The Jewish calendar is dated from a time nearly 6,000 years ago, when people of that faith believe that the creation of the world took place. The Jewish year 5760 ends on September 29, 2000. So the seventh Jewish millennium is not due for another 240 years.

The Hindu calendar is also very old. It was based on the movement of the Sun and the Moon and was also divided into "eras." Different parts of India had different calendars. Because of this the government of India decided to introduce a new official calendar.

6

This began on the Western date of March 22, 1957, which was the year 1878 on the Hindu calendar. The Western year 2000 begins in the Hindu year 1921. The Islamic calendar is the most recent. It is dated from the Western year 622. But each Islamic year is about ten days shorter than the Western year. The Western year 2000 begins during the Islamic year 1420.

The Christian calendar begins with the supposed date of the birth of Jesus Christ. The letters A.D. are often put before the number of the year. This stands for *Anno Domini*, which is Latin for "in the year of the Lord." Years before the birth of Christ have B.C. after them, meaning "before Christ."

works mark the beginning of a Year in Singapore. Such dramatic brations will be seen the world over e beginning of the year 2000.

THE WESTERN MILLENNIUM

Millions of people worldwide will celebrate January 1, 2000. There will be parties on New Year's Eve. Then, at midnight, the new millennium will arrive. But is this true? Some say it is not. After all there was no year A.D. 0. The first "year of the Lord" was A.D. 1. Two thousand years will not really have passed until December 2000. So the new millennium should not start until January 1, 2001. However, all Western countries have decided to celebrate the arrival of the year 2000—in itself a special moment in history.

Over the past 1,000 years, many people have made predictions about what will happen at the millennium. Let us look at what some of them have said and written.

Prophecies of Nostradamus

Some people have tried to predict what will happen in the year 2000. Many old prophecies have already come true.

This painting (opposite) shows the great French doctor and astrologer Nostradamus. We have yet to see if all his predictions will come true.

Michel de Nostredame was a French doctor. He is usually called Nostradamus, which is his name in Latin. He was born at St. Rémy, in southeastern France, in 1503. He studied medicine at the university of Montpellier and later became well-known for his treatment of people suffering from the bubonic plague. Nostradamus was also an astrologer, or someone who studies the movements of the stars and planets in relation to each other. From these studies, astrologers try to predict the future. In 1555 Nostradamus first published an unusual book called *Centuries*.

Centuries is a collection of verses, each of four lines. They are called quatrains. The verses use wordplay and all sorts of code words. The quatrains were first published in groups of 100 verses—the "centuries."

IMPORTANT DATES

It is difficult to understand the quatrains, and no two experts can agree on the meaning of most of them. Because they were badly printed, even some of the words are difficult to make out. However, many books have been written in an attempt to explain them.

In 1555 Nostradamus first published an unusual book called Centuries.

Nostradamus became famous during his own life-time because he correctly predicted the death of the French King, Henry II, in 1559. Many of the verses are thought to be about powerful men and women who were alive in Nostradamus's time. Some, however, seem to predict events far into the future.

Nostradamus mentions specific dates in only a few quatrains. Two are particularly important. One is in verse 72, in "Century 10." Nostradamus wrote:

The year 1999, and seven months:
A great King of Terror will come from the sky
To revive the great king of the Mongols.
Before and after, Mars reigns for a time.

What does this mean? Nostradamus seems certain about the date—July 1999. "Mars" means war. More than one writer about Nostradamus has compared this verse to the science fiction book *The War of the*

In 1559 King Henry II was killed at a tournament. A lance went through his helmet into his brain. Nostradamus had predicted this three years earlier.

This is part of an altar decoration in a church. It shows the dead rising to heaven from their graves.

Worlds, by the English writer H. G. Wells. In this book Wells describes how Earth is taken over by alien beings from the planet Mars. Many people thought Nostradamus must have meant that a man from Mars would come to Earth. However, scientists are now almost certain that there is no present life on Mars. But what about "the great king of the Mongols"? Can this mean the modern power of China?

Nostradamus wrote at a time in history when the end of the world was expected in A.D. 2000. But in quatrain number 74 he wrote:

When Time has turned to the seventh millennium,
Then will come the sacrifice of many victims,
Not long from the Great Millennium,
When those in their graves will emerge.

This seems to refer to the Jewish year 7000, that is, the fall of the Western year A.D. 2039. According to many faiths, the dead will all rise from their graves when the world ends. At last, it is said, there will be great peace and happiness.

Perhaps Nostradamus did not expect the world to end in A.D. 1999, but in the Jewish year 7000. This is one example of how difficult it is to understand the true meaning of Nostradamus's writings.

EVENTS IN THE FUTURE

In 1938 Dr. Max de Fontbrune published a book. It gave his understanding of the verses of Nostradamus. Explaining one of the verses, de Fontbrune wrote that Germany would soon be at war with France. He also said that the German army would enter France through Belgium. In the end Germany would be defeated, and their leader, Adolf Hitler, would die. All this came true. De Fontbrune had been right.

. . . Nostradamus had written about the outbreak of World War III in 1999.

Max de Fontbrune's son, Jean-Charles, continued his father's work. In 1980 he published a book that examined Nostradamus's quatrains. Nearly half the book described events that were still to come. Jean-Charles claimed that Nostradamus had written about the outbreak of World War III in 1999. He said Nostradamus had described the use of nuclear warheads and the death or capture of 300,000 soldiers. Pope John Paul II, de Fontbrune said, would be forced to flee from Italy when the Russians invaded. He went on to say that the pope would be killed by an assassin at Lyon, in France.

MANY TRUE WORDS

De Fontbrune also said Nostradamus had predicted trouble in the Arab world. The Arab Moslems would come to an agreement with the Russians. Iraq would attack the West. There would be great revolutions in several countries. The Soviet Union would break up, and Moslem troops would occupy Italy. The French government would fall. Soon all the countries of western Europe would be occupied, and then the Moslems and Chinese would join forces. Could de Fontbrune's description of such a world war have been what Nostradamus meant in his quatrain 72?

Since de Fontbrune's book was published, several of the predictions he described have certainly come true. The Soviet Union has broken up. Iraq has been at war with the West. However, these events took place before the year 1999. Thankfully, they are not the result of a major world war. Although the world is still not truly at peace, great efforts are being made by various governments to make people talk rather than fight. As a result many more of de Fontbrune's predictions appear less likely—but who can be sure what will happen in the next millennium?

The new Russian flag is proudly displayed in Red Square on August 22, 1991. The Soviet Union finally broke up on December 31, 1991. Had Nostradamus predicted this in his quatrains?

The Great Pyramid

The great pyramids of Egypt are said to hold many secrets. But can they tell us when the world will end?

Two men pray in front of the ancient Sphinx and the Great Pyramid in Egypt (opposite). These great monuments have always been thought to have mysterious powers.

One of the Seven Wonders of the Ancient World lies some ten miles to the southwest of Cairo, in Egypt. This is the Great Pyramid of the pharaoh Khufu—the Greeks called him Cheops, and this name is still sometimes used. The base covers 13 acres (5 hectares), and it is nearly 500 feet (152 m) tall. It is thought to have been built sometime around 2500 B.C.

Inside the pyramid are several chambers, or large rooms, which are connected by passages known as galleries. It was once believed that the pyramid had been built as a tomb for Khufu. However, there is no proof that his body was ever laid to rest there.

PROPHECY OF THE PYRAMID

One of the first Europeans to make measurements of the Great Pyramid was John Greaves. He was a professor of math at Oxford University in England. In 1638 he traveled to Egypt. He later wrote a book about the pyramid. In this book Greaves described an Egyptian legend that said the pyramid contained records of "what is, and what shall be, from the beginning of time, to the end of it."

14

. . . the pyramid contained . . . "what is, and what shall be, from the beginning of time, to the end of it."

During the 19th century, an Englishman named John Taylor became interested in the Great Pyramid. He never visited Egypt. Instead he built himself a model of the pyramid and studied it. He was sure that the measurements of the Great Pyramid recorded the size of the planet Earth and the length of the year. A respected Scottish scientist, Professor Piazzi-Smyth, was extremely interested in Taylor's findings.

In 1864, Piazzi-Smyth went to Egypt. He wanted to see if he could find out more about the mysterious powers of the Great Pyramid. He found that Taylor's measurements from the model pyramid matched those of the real pyramid. Besides, Piazzi-Smyth thought that some of his own measurements showed all kinds of other facts about the Earth and the universe, including the distance of Earth from the Sun.

PREDICTING THE END OF THE WORLD

Many scientists laughed at such an unlikely claim. However, others remembered the legend that the pyramid contained records "from the beginning of time, to the end of it."

. . . the measurements . . . recorded the size of the Earth and the length of the year.

These scientists decided that the Great Pyramid actually told the whole history of the human race—from the beginning to the still unknown end. They used the measurements of the galleries and chambers to represent years, months, and days. Taking the date

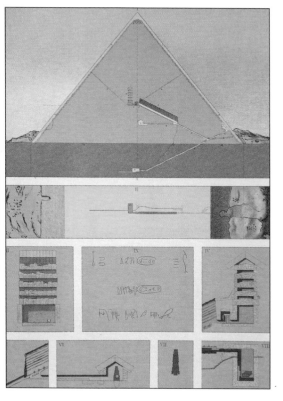

This 19th-century drawing shows some of the chambers and passages that were found inside of the Great Pyramid.

of the world's creation as 4000 B.C., they predicted that the end of the world would come at midsummer 2045. It was a terrible prediction for the new millennium.

People who believed this became known as "pyramidologists." One leading pyramidologist was Englishman David Davidson. In 1924 he published his findings. Among his measurements he found that the length of one of the passages in the Great Pyramid could be used to represent the period of time from August 4, 1914, to November 11, 1918. This was the length of World War I. Davidson, however, also worked out that the last date represented by the measurements in the pyramid was September 17, 2001. Could this mean that the world would end during the first year of the new millennium?

THE WORLD'S GREATEST MYSTERY

Pyramidologists have found some measurements in the Great Pyramid that they claim to be able to tie to every important event in past history. The one thing they cannot agree on, however, is when the end of the world will actually happen.

Predictions of Edgar Cayce

Cayce was an unusual healer. But he was also able to see into the future.

Edgar Cayce was born in Kentucky in 1877. When he was seven years old, he had a dream. In this dream he was asked what he would most like to do with his life. He replied that he would like to help the sick.

Some years later Cayce discovered that he had special healing powers. As an adult, he began to treat the sick. He would lie down on a couch and go into a type of deep sleep. While in this sleeplike state, he was able to "see" what was wrong with his patients. He then described treatments to cure them. When he died in 1945, Cayce left records of more than 15,000 cases that he had successfully treated over 43 years.

SEEING THE FUTURE

The streets of New York on October 30, 1929 (opposite). It was the day after the great Wall Street Crash, when millions of people lost their life savings.

Cayce, however, was not only famous for his unusual healing powers. He could also see into the future. Months before it happened, Cayce had predicted the Wall Street stock-market crash of October 1929. In 1939 he said that two U.S. presidents would die while they were still in office. Franklin D. Roosevelt died early in his third term, in 1945. John F. Kennedy was shot and killed by an assassin in 1963.

Months before it happened, Cayce had predicted the Wall Street stock-market crash of October 1929.

In 1934 Cayce made a number of predictions about the years leading up to the millennium. First, he said, there would be earthquakes in Los Angeles and San Francisco. Parts of California would fall into the sea. After this, disaster would hit the East Coast of the United States. New York City would disappear, as well as parts of South Carolina and Georgia.

"The greater portion of Japan," said Cayce, "must go into the sea."

There would be terrible floods in Mississippi, Missouri, and Louisiana. Then the Great Lakes would empty into the Gulf of Mexico. At the same time, new land would rise from the ocean off the southeast coast. However, said Cayce, parts of the eastern U.S. would be safe: "Safety lands will be in the area around Norfolk, Virginia Beach, parts of Ohio, Indiana, and Illinois, and much of the southern and east portions of Canada. Norfolk is to be a mighty good place, and a safe place. . . ."

RING OF FIRE

Volcanic activity would be massive in the so-called "Ring of Fire." This is an area of the Pacific Ocean that includes Japan, China, Southeast Asia, eastern Australia, and South America. "The greater portion of Japan," said Cayce, "must go into the sea." He went on to predict that the explosion of volcanoes would be caused by huge earthquakes in both the Arctic and the Antarctic. He said that the northern part of Europe would be changed "in the twinkling of an eye." According to Cayce, "Moss and ferns will grow" in the present frozen areas of the world, and "open waters will appear in Greenland."

Although on a smaller scale than Cayce supposed, some of the predictions that he made for the years leading up to the millennium have already come true. In California and Japan, there have been earthquakes. Much of the world has suffered serious flooding.

Experts still await Cayce's predicted earthquakes that will change the world forever. However, some scientists have said that volcanoes on Hawaii could cause a huge rockslide into the ocean. This would send a wave of water, more than 16 feet (4.8 m) high, across the Pacific Ocean. It would flood the east coast of Japan and drive a wall of water far inland into the Australian state of Queensland. There could still be time for Cayce's prediction to come true.

This is volcanic lava flowing into a crater in the Hawaii Volcanoes National Park. Edgar Cayce believed that exploding volcanoes would lead to world disaster in the new millennium.

The Bible Code

Using computers, some people claim to have found predictions for the future in the Bible.

The first five books of the Bible are known in English as Genesis, Exodus, Leviticus, Numbers, and Deuteronomy. These are very old Jewish writings that were originally written in Hebrew. In Hebrew they are called the Torah. Over the centuries, many people have come up with the idea that there might be a code in the Bible that predicts the course of all human history.

HIDDEN MEANING

More than 50 years ago an amazing discovery was made by a rabbi (a Jewish religious leader). He found, at the very beginning of Genesis, that every fiftieth Hebrew letter spelled out the word *Torah*. He found the same thing to be true in Exodus, Numbers, and Deuteronomy.

Dr. Eliyahu Rips heard about this discovery for the first time around 1980. He is a world-famous mathematician and believes that he has found many prophecies hidden in the Bible. He decided to write a computer program to search through the Torah for patterns or codes.

Rips was helped by Doron Witztum. The two men listed 32 famous thinkers, from ancient to modern times. They fed the names of these wise

A Torah lies open on the altar in the Great Synagogue in Jerusalem, Israel (opposite).

22

Over the centuries, many people have come up with the idea that there might be a code in the Bible. . . .

people into the computer, together with their birth and death dates. Then, they instructed the computer to sort through the words of the Torah to see if it contained these names and dates.

Amazingly the computer found the letters and figures of each name and date close together. Dr. Rips worked out that the chance of this happening by accident was one in 10 million—in other words, it was no accident.

The computer came up with the words war, enemy, Saddam . . . and fire. . . .

Harold Gans was an experienced codebreaker at the National Security Agency. He heard about this discovery and decided to write his own computer program. There were the names and the dates. Gans then searched for the cities where the wise men had been born and died. He found these as well.

DETECTIVE WORK

A computer reads each space between words as if it were an extra letter. Dr. Rips cut out all the word spaces. Then he asked the computer to search for letters that were an equal number of letters apart. Here is a simple example of how the code works.

Starting at the first letter, read every fourth letter in the following sentence, up to and including the word *every*: "Rips explained that each code is a case of adding every fourth, or twelfth, or fiftieth letter to form a word."

If you have done it correctly, the letters spell out the message "read the code." Dr. Rips searched for messages in the same way.

The computer came up with the words *war, enemy, Saddam, Hussein picked a day, missile,* and *fire on 3rd Shebat.* The 3rd Shebat is the date in the Jewish calendar that is the same as January 18, 1991, in the Western World. During the Gulf War, Iraq fired its first missile at Israel on January 18, 1991. Dr. Rips had found his message just three weeks earlier!

ANOTHER TERRIBLE PREDICTION

Michael Drosnin is an American journalist. He went to Jerusalem to interview Dr. Rips. Rips showed him a report that had been accepted by the leading U.S. math journal, *Statistical Science.* Three different experts agreed that Rips's discoveries were true. Rips and Drosnin decided to look in the Torah for *Yitzhak Rabin.* He was Prime Minister of Israel at that time.

Boys on an anti-American march in Baghdad, Iraq. They are holding pictures of Saddam Hussein. The computer came up with his name in December 1990.

25

To make the messages easier to read, the computer arranges the letters of the Torah in rows, one above the other. Searching for *Yitzhak Rabin*, it printed out 64 rows. There, in a column of seven Hebrew letters, was the name. But, even more surprisingly, there was a message across. It read *assassin will assassinate*. Another search came up with a date close by. It was the Jewish year 5756, which began in September 1995. On November 4, 1995, Rabin was shot dead. Afterward, Rips looked

Israeli Prime Minister Benjamin Netanyahu, on the right, at a meeting in 1996.

at his computer printout again. There, just two lines above Rabin's name, was the name of the assassin.

WARNINGS FOR THE MILLENNIUM

Searching for hidden meanings in the Torah is not new. Many Jewish experts have studied the writings over the centuries. Nevertheless, Dr. Rips's discovery is amazing. He claims that all human history has been written in code in the Torah. So, he says, it must predict what is coming in the future. However, because nobody knows the names of people who are not yet born, it is hard to search for coming events.

As a starting point, Rips and Drosnin looked for the name of another well-known person. In May 1996, they found *Prime Minister Netanyahu*, his nickname *Bibi*, and *elected*. A week later, Benjamin Netanyahu was elected Israeli Prime Minister. But across his name ran the message *surely he will be killed*. Drosnin is sure that this will happen.

Because Dr. Rips is an Israeli, he and Drosnin have limited their search of the Torah to things related to Israel. Drosnin has written a book, *The Bible Code*, about their work. He says that they found the words *atomic, the next war,* and *it will be after the death of the Prime Minister.* Close by, says Drosnin, they found the year 5760—in the Western calendar 1999-2000. There were also the names *Libya* and *Syria.*

WORLD WAR III

Drosnin's discovery is alarming. He wrote, ". . . that is how World War III might begin—with an atomic attack on Jerusalem, followed by" Israel being entered by force. Drosnin also predicts earthquakes in 2000, 2006, 2010, and 2113. Some time between 2000 and 2006, he says, a huge earthquake will strike Japan, and also China. In 2010 a major earthquake will hit Los Angeles.

In his book Drosnin ends by saying: "Is the Bible code merely giving a [look of true science to the excitement over the new millennium]—or is it warning us . . . of a very real danger? There is no way to know. The code may be neither 'right' nor 'wrong.' It probably tells us what might happen, not what will happen. But since we cannot let our world be destroyed, we cannot simply wait —we must [suppose] that the warning in the Bible code is real."

A pointer in the shape of a golden hand is used to help read a Torah. Do these letters really hold a hidden code?

Looking to the Skies

People interested in astrology will tell you that we are entering the Age of Aquarius. This, they say, will be a new age of peace and understanding. But what is the Age of Aquarius?

The study of astrology began some 4,000 years ago. In the night sky, people could see the Moon and five planets. We now call these planets Venus, Mercury, Mars, Jupiter, and Saturn. In ancient times people watched the planets, and the Sun and Moon, moving through the skies and believed they influenced our lives. Astrology developed as a way of trying to predict what was going to happen next.

THE ZODIAC

The planets, the Sun, and the Moon could be seen moving—day by day, or month by month—against the background of the stars. The pattern of the stars also moved. Over the course of a year the stars returned to the same position.

At the same time each year, the Sun appeared in the same position among the same group of stars. People thought that each group of stars—what we call a constellation—looked like an animal. During one year the Sun seems to move

This 16th-century picture shows a man looking up into space at the Sun, Moon, stars, and planets (opposite).

In ancient times people watched the planets . . . and believed they influenced our lives.

through a circle of constellations. The Greeks called this the zodiac, which means "circle of animals."

At springtime, 4,000 years ago, the Sun was seen to be moving across the constellation called Aries, the Ram. This occurred around the date we now call March 21. This is the day in spring when there are exactly 12 hours between sunrise and sunset, and 12 hours between sunset and dawn. It is called the equinox, which means "equal night." Everything else that had anything to do with the stars and planets was worked out from this date.

THE AGE OF AQUARIUS

But something strange was slowly happening. Astrologers did not discover this for some time. As we now know, the Earth makes a complete turn every day. It turns on its axis, or central point, which runs between the North and South poles. At the same time, it is wobbling very slightly, like a spinning top that is slowing down. So, gradually, the axis is making a small circle. It takes nearly 26,000 years to make this circle.

Because of this the stars slowly seem to alter their position. By about 2,000 years ago, the Sun was no longer entering Aries at the end of March. It was moving back through the zodiac.

This is an old print titled Harmonia Macrocosmica. *It is a map showing all the different signs of the zodiac.*

It had left Aries and was moving across the constellation of Pisces, the Fishes. Over the last 2,000 years, the Sun has gradually passed across the constellation Pisces. Soon in the new millennium, it will appear to enter Aquarius, the Water Carrier, around March 23. This is called "the dawning of the Age of Aquarius."

... the first years of the millennium will be filled with natural disasters ...

However, this slow change has not been noticed by most astrologers. They still draw horoscopes with the Sun moving across Aries around March 21. It is also thought to be unimportant by many astronomers. Astrologers study the movements of the stars and planets in relation to each other in order to predict the future. Astronomers study the stars and planets, as well as their movements, for scientific reasons.

AGE OF PEACE?

Most astrologers agree that the Age of Aquarius will be one of peace and greater understanding among humankind. This is something like the "golden age" that was predicted 500 years ago for the millennium. On the other hand, some people predict that the first years of the millennium will be filled with natural disasters such as earthquakes and floods.

We know how the positions of the Sun and Moon affect the tides of the oceans. When the Sun and Moon are together on the same side of the Earth, or on opposite sides, the tides are at their highest. When

These photographs show Mont-Saint-Michel, off the coast of Normandy, France. The island was completely cut off at high tide before the 3,000 foot (900 meter) causeway, or raised road, was built (left). It is possible to walk across the sand to the island at low tide (right).

the Sun and Moon are at right angles to each other, the tides are lowest. This happens because the force of gravity from the Sun and Moon actually pulls the water toward them. Perhaps, some people say, this force also affects other things on Earth. Some think that the planets, too, may have a similar effect.

Normally people would not notice if they had. Usually the planets are all at different positions around the Earth. But every now and then they are close together in the same area of sky. This will happen early in the new millennium. Some scientists have predicted that it could produce terrible floods and earthquakes.

PLANET PREDICTIONS

In May 2000, five planets will have moved around in space, so that they are close together on one side of the Sun—on the opposite side from the Earth. This is similar to the position of the Sun and Moon that produces high tides. Some scientists have suggested that this will even have an effect on the Sun itself.

All kinds of strange things happen on the Sun. There are fierce storms that affect radio reception on Earth. Neutrinos, which are tiny particles from the Sun, shower down on Earth. Nobody knows what effect they have on living things. Also, there are the darker areas of the Sun called sunspots.

UNKNOWN FUTURE

Sunspots move freely around the surface of the Sun. Sometimes only a few of them appear at the same time. Other times there are many more. The oddest fact about sunspots is that they act like magnets—they draw things toward them. However, every now and then the magnetism changes. This causes the sunspots to push things away.

Some people say that the position of the planets in May 2000 will produce a great many sunspots. Some scientists who study the structure of the Earth believe this might cause the Earth's own gravity, or natural magnetic force, to change. If it did, the effects on the planet could be really disastrous.

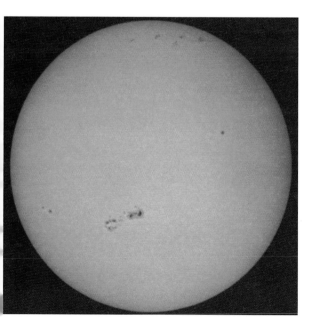

This is photograph of the Sun. It was taken using special filters. You should never look directly at the Sun without protection. The dark areas are sunspots.

33

Other Prophets

Saints, palmists, and the great books of the Bible have all predicted events in the future.

Malachy was an Irish monk. He was born in Ulster, the northern part of Ireland, in 1094. In 1138 he set out for Rome to ask the pope to appoint an archbishop in Ireland. An archbishop is an important leader in some Christian churches. In those days people had to travel on horseback, or on foot. It took many months to travel from Ireland to Italy. When he reached France, Malachy stayed for a while at the Abbey of Clairvaux before continuing his journey. When Malachy finally arrived in Rome he was welcomed by the pope, Innocent II. Malachy hoped the pope would name him as the new Irish archbishop. But instead the pope ordered Malachy to return to Ireland.

THE MAKING OF A SAINT

Churches on the slopes of the Mount of Olives in Jerusalem (opposite). There is a connection between this place and Malachy's prophecy that the next pope will have been born a Jew.

Pope Innocent II died in 1143. Over the next few years there was trouble in the Roman Church. Many people had different ideas about who should be the next pope. In 1145, Pope Eugenius III was finally elected. While on a trip to France he, too, decided to stay at Clairvaux Abbey. Malachy heard of this, and in October 1148 he arrived at the Abbey. He hoped, once

The olive tree is the symbol of Jerusalem. The Mount of Olives is found there.

again, to be made the Irish archbishop. However, before any decision had been made, Malachy died on November 3. Later, he was named a saint.

Saint Malachy is supposed to have left a series of prophecies among his papers at Clairvaux Abbey. They were about future popes. However, nothing was heard of these prophecies for nearly 450 years. Then, in 1595, a monk named Arnold de Wion said that he had read Malachy's prophecies. Later, De Wion wrote about what Malachy had said in a book, *The Prophecies of Saint Malachy*.

THE FUTURE POPES

Malachy's prophecies do not name the future popes. Instead, each pope is described by a few words. The 112 descriptions are written in Latin. Amazingly,

A view of Venice. The man who was pope from 1958 to 1963 had been head of the church in Venice, which is surrounded by water. Malachy described him as "Shepherd and Seaman."

This is Pope John Paul II during a visit to Brazil. He was the first pope to visit South America. Malachy had described him as "Labor of the Sun."

Malachy seems to have identified small, personal things to do with every pope since 1143. Here are just a few examples.

Alexander IV, pope from 1254 to 1261, was described by the words *Signum Ostiense* "the Sign of Ostia." In fact, he had been a churchman in Ostia, the seaport of Rome. Leo XIII was pope from 1878 to 1903. Malachy called him *Lumen in Caelo* "Light in the Heavens"—this could relate to his family's coat of arms, or special symbol, which included a comet. It would seem that both Malachy's prophecies had come true. And there were others.

Pope John XXIII (1958-63) was described by the words *Pastor et Nauta* "Shepherd and Seaman." He had, in fact, been the head of the church in Venice. This is the Italian city built on marshy ground in the middle of a lagoon, a type of shallow lake. Again, Malachy's description seemed to be correct.

John Paul I was pope for only 34 days. Malachy had described him as *De Medietate Lunae* "of the Half Moon." Strangely, he died on September 28, 1978, when only half the moon could be seen. Malachy's description of Pope John Paul II, was *De Labore Solis*. This means "Labor of the Sun." Perhaps this refers to the fact that he was the first pope to visit and work in the hot countries of Latin America.

A MILLENNIUM POPE

So what did St. Malachy have to say about the millennium? His 111th motto is *De Gloria Olivae* "of the Glory of the Olive Tree." The olive tree is the symbol of Jerusalem. The Mount of Olives is found there. Many people think that Malachy's prophecy means the next pope will have been born a Jew. Experts think he will be Jean-Marie Lustiger, the present French Cardinal. He was born to a Jewish mother in Poland in 1926—and not far from his birthplace is a little town called Oliva!

. . . there would be many changes with the approach of the . . . new millennium.

WAR AND PEACE

Louis Hamon was another famous Irish prophet. He was born in Wicklow, in the eastern part of Ireland, in 1866, he became famous as a palmist—someone who claims to be able to tell what a person is like and what the future holds by looking at the lines on his or her hands. He was known as Cheiro.

This is the room in London where the famous palmist Cheiro read people's hands. It had carpets on the ceilings and walls. Many of the objects in the room were from all over the world.

As a palmist, Cheiro made many successful readings of people's hands. Then, in 1931, he published a book titled *Cheiro's World Predictions*. In the book he wrote that there would be many changes with the approach of the "Age of Aquarius" in the new millennium. He said there would be terrible wars, and that people would go hungry. He said that kings and queens would be overthrown by the people. It would be the death of the "old" world and the birth of the "new."

However, Cheiro went on to say that after the times of trouble and war, the "new" world would slowly become better. He wrote, ". . . that in the end seeds may have more richness, flowers more fullness, and all sections of humanity [people] more love for one another."

39

Cheiro predicted that during the new millennium the major religious groups of the world, such as the Catholics, Christians, Jews, Muslims, and Hindus, would break up. For a time there would be hundreds of different smaller religious groups with their own beliefs. Then, slowly, they would all combine into a single world religion.

CHANGES FOR WOMEN

He also predicted that the role of women in society would change. Instead of having no choice but to stay at home and look after the children, women would be able to go out to work and earn their own money. Cheiro said that this would slowly lead to men treating women as their equals. "Even in such old civilizations as China and Japan . . . women will everywhere throw off their shackles" and chains.

An Iraqi soldier during the Iran-Iraq War of 1980-1988. Prophets in centuries gone by said that there would be a great war in the East in the millennium.

The world has had several ice ages in its history. In recent years, many parts of the world are having increasingly cold winters. Could this be the beginning of Cheiro's predicted ice age?

Another of Cheiro's predictions for the future suggests that World War III might break out at the turn of the 21st century. This was also one prophecy that Eliyahu Rips and Michael Drosnin claimed to have found in code in the Torah during their research in 1996. In his book Cheiro said that a great battle would be fought in Palestine, present-day Israel. He described how "the people of the North" would invade the country "with allies drawn from Iran, Ethiopia, Libya, and many [other] people."

CHANGING CLIMATE

In 1934 American psychic Edgar Cayce had warned of huge changes in the world's climate in the new millennium. Cheiro also predicted such changes in climate. He said that there would be a new ice age

41

in Europe. Ireland, Great Britain, Sweden, Norway, Denmark, the northern parts of Russia, Germany, France, and Spain would gradually become too cold for people to live there anymore.

"Then I saw a new Heaven and a new Earth; for the first Heaven and the first Earth had passed away. . . ."

THE REVELATION

Cheiro went on to say that hot countries, such as India and Egypt, and other African nations, would cool down and enjoy a climate much like that of Northern Europe today. As a result, there would be an increase in the numbers of people living in all these countries.

ANCIENT WRITINGS

The prophecies of Edgar Cayce and Cheiro—and many others—are clearly connected to an ancient book known as The Revelation or The Apocalypse. This is the last book in the Bible. The word *apocalypse* comes from Greek, and means "that which is revealed." The book was written nearly 2,000 years ago. Nobody knows who wrote it, but many say it was written by St. John.

The book is full of strange, frightening descriptions. The Devil is described as being a great red dragon, "with seven heads and ten horns." There are four horsemen, the last of whom is said to be "Death, on a pale horse." And there is a beast—

"like a leopard, and his feet were like the feet of a bear, and his mouth like the mouth of a lion." The Revelation describes all kinds of terrible things that will happen to the world.

WORDS OF HOPE

Then, toward the end, comes what is probably the best-known part in the book. It describes what will happen at the end of the world: "Then I saw a new Heaven and a new Earth; for the first Heaven and the first Earth had passed away, and the sea was no more. . . . and I heard a great voice . . . saying . . . 'the dwelling [home] of God is with men. He will dwell [live] with them . . . he will wipe away every tear from their eyes, and death shall be no more, neither shall there be . . . pain any more, for the former things have passed away.'"

In The Revelation, the Devil is said to be a red dragon "with seven heads and ten horns." Here, angels prepare to fight the fire-breathing monster.

Modern Predictions

Noel Tyl is a well-known American astrologer. In 1996 he published a book titled *Predictions for a New Millennium*. Tyl claims that all his predictions are based on the positions of the planets. He worked out where they would be on certain dates in the 21st century. He said this meant he could tell what would happen in the future.

ANOTHER PRESIDENTIAL TRAGEDY

One of Tyl's predictions is that another U.S. president will be assassinated. This will happen around the year 2004. This is an election year. The danger period is from March 2003 through December 2005. So the president at the time may die before his or her term is up, most likely between March 28 and June 15, 2004. Or it may be that the newly elected president will be killed between February and April 2005.

Tyl says that the killing of the president could be linked to the Middle East. He predicts that the U.S. Army will be sent to take over the Golan Heights, the high hills on the border between Israel and Syria. Around the same time, Saddam Hussein will be overthrown in Iraq. U.S. forces will be called in to keep the peace.

The Golan Heights (opposite) were captured by Israel during the Arab-Israeli War of 1967. Noel Tyl predicts that the U.S. Army will control the area in the new millennium.

44

. . . the U.S. Army will be sent to take over the Golan Heights.

CHANGES IN THE EAST

In the Far East, Tyl predicts great changes. Japan will apologize for attacking the U.S. in 1941. Following this, the Japanese government will lose the support of its people. This may result in some kind of military rule. However, by the spring of 2008, says Tyl, the Japanese state will be trouble free once more.

New trading agreements will be made between China and Japan. This will come as a result of China's giving up communism. The move away from communism will begin in the fall of 1999. After this, North and South Korea will become one country sometime between April 2003 and September 2004. At the same time, there will big changes in the Philippines. By the beginning of the year 2003, most eastern parts of the world will have become richer than they have ever been before.

EUROPEAN DEVELOPMENTS

For Europe Tyl also makes a number of predictions. The French president, Jacques Chirac, will give up his position, probably in January 2000. His reason may well be sickness. Charles, the English Prince of Wales, will never become king. Instead, his older son, William, will succeed Queen Elizabeth II sometime between September 2001 and March 2002.

Tyl's predictions are extremely interesting. They are also somewhat comforting. Unlike some of the prophecies mentioned in earlier chapters, he does not appear to predict the ending of the world in the millennium. Perhaps his most amazing prediction is his statement that the United States will make the first contact with beings from outer space—possibly in the late summer of the year 2004!

Glossary

allies Countries that agree to help each other in times of war.

assassin A person who kills people for money, or for political reasons.

astrological Anything to do with the movements of stars and planets.

astrology The study of the movements of the stars and planets and their influence on human lives.

atomic Using nuclear energy. Nuclear energy is produced if the central part, or nucleus, of an atom is split or joined to another atom.

bubonic plague A deadly disease spread by fleas.

civilization Advanced human development in a particular time or place. "The Aztec civilization."

coat of arms Patterns or pictures in a shieldlike shape. Used as a symbol by families or universities.

comet A ball of ice, dust, and chunks of rock that orbits the Sun.

elected Voted into a position of power by the people.

era A long period of time.

gravity (Earth's) A natural force that pulls things toward Earth.

horoscope A person's future. Based on the position of the stars and planets at the time of birth.

hypnotist A person who puts others into a sleeplike state.

ice age A period of time when Earth was covered with ice.

infection Disease caused by germs.

lava Hot, liquid rock.

magnetism The ability to attract. For example, a magnet's power.

milestone A very important event.

millennium An era of 1,000 years.

pharaoh A king of ancient Egypt.

prediction The description of an event before it actually happens.

prophecies The telling of what will happen in the future. Based on feelings rather than scientific fact.

prophet A person who predicts what will happen in the future.

prosperity Great success. Usually to do with wealth or good fortune.

psychic A person who claims to be able to see into the future, or who has other unexplained powers of the mind.

revolutions The overthrow of a country's government by force.

volcanic activity The explosive throwing out of lava, ash, and gases from a volcano.

Index

Further Reading

Cush, Cathie. *Disasters That Shook the World*, "Twenty Events" series. Raintree Steck-Vaughn, 1993

Ross, Stewart. *Arab-Israeli Conflict*, "Causes and Consequences" series. Raintree Steck-Vaughn, 1996

Royer, Mary P. *Astrology: Opposing Viewpoints*, "Great Mysteries" series. Greenhaven, 1991

Spellman, Linda. *Codes*, "Enrichment & Gifted" series. Learning Works, 1992

Tremaine, John. *Astrology and Predictions*, "Workstations" series. Price Stern Sloan, 1996